Orange Line 1

Vokabellernheft

Herausgeber: Dr. Frank Haß

Ernst Klett Verlag
Stuttgart • Leipzig

Liebe Schülerin, lieber Schüler,

mit diesem Vokabellernheft im praktischen Taschenformat kannst du überall deine Wörter lernen, wiederholen und nachschlagen.
In den Wortlisten kannst du Wörter und Wendungen, die dir schwierig vorkommen, mit Textmarker oder Bleistift markieren, um sie dann immer wieder durchzugehen.
Auch die vielen Übungen nach jeder Unit unterstützen dich bei der Wiederholung. So kannst du dich prima auf Vokabeltests vorbereiten.

In den Übungen, die mit diesem Zeichen ● gekennzeichnet sind, übst du die blau gedruckten Wörter.

Hinter jedem Wort ist die Lautschrift (z. B. [heləʊ] für *Hello!*) angegeben. Diese hilft dir, wenn du nicht weißt, wie du das Wort aussprechen sollst.
Hilfreiche Hinweise zum Umgang mit den Lautschriftzeichen findest du **in deinem Englischbuch** auf Seite 183 und ab Seite 236 am unteren Rand aller *Dictionary*-Seiten.

Viel Erfolg beim Vokabellernen!

Welcome – Hello!

p. 8	**welcome (to)** ['welkəm (tʊ)]	willkommen (bei/in)
	Hello. [hə'ləʊ]	Hallo.
	I'm (= I am) [aɪm]	ich bin
	the [ðə]	der; die *(auch Pl.)*; das
	bat [bæt]	Fledermaus
	Nice to meet you. [ˌnaɪs tə 'mi:t ju:]	Nett, dich kennen zu lernen.
	What's your name? [ˌwɒts jə 'neɪm]	Wie heißt du?
	I like [aɪ 'laɪk]	ich mag
	English ['ɪŋglɪʃ]	englisch; Englisch; aus England
	Hi. [haɪ]	Hi.; Hallo.
	My name is ... [maɪ 'neɪm‿ɪz]	Ich heiße ...
	Hello there. [hə'ləʊ ˌðeə]	Hallo.; Grüß dich.
	music ['mju:zɪk]	Musik
	And you? [ænd 'ju:]	Und du?
	sport [spɔ:t]	Sport
	animal ['ænɪml]	Tier
	computer [ˌkəm'pju:tə]	Computer
	It's time to go. [ɪts ˌtaɪm tə 'gəʊ]	Es ist Zeit zu gehen.
	See you later. [ˌsi: jə 'leɪtə]	Tschüss.; Bis bald.
	yes [jes]	ja
	Bye. [baɪ]	Tschüss.
	Goodbye. [gʊd'baɪ]	Auf Wiedersehen.
	See you. ['si: ju:]	Tschüss.; Bis bald.

numbers

zero 0 ['zɪərəʊ]	null	**six 6** [sɪks]	sechs
one 1 [wʌn]	eins	**seven 7** ['sevn]	sieben
two 2 [tu:]	zwei	**eight 8** [eɪt]	acht
three 3 [θri:]	drei	**nine 9** [naɪn]	neun
four 4 [fɔ:]	vier	**ten 10** [ten]	zehn
five 5 [faɪv]	fünf		

Zoom in – In a park

p. 10	**in** [ɪn]	in
	a [ə]	ein, eine
	park [pɑ:k]	Park
	colour ['kʌlə]	Farbe
	activity [æk'tɪvəti]	Aktivität
	number ['nʌmbə]	Nummer; Zahl
	people *(pl)* ['pi:pl]	Leute; Menschen
	dog [dɒg]	Hund
	tennis ['tenɪs]	Tennis
	boy [bɔɪ]	Junge
p. 11	**I spy with my little eye …** [aɪ spaɪ wɪð ˌmaɪ lɪtl 'aɪ]	Ich sehe was, was du nicht siehst …
	something ['sʌmθɪŋ]	etwas
	it's (= it is) [ɪts]	es ist
	here [hɪə]	hier
	bus [bʌs]	Bus
	I can play football. [ˌaɪ kən ˌpleɪ 'fʊtbɔ:l]	Ich kann Fußball spielen.
	I can buy … [aɪ kən 'baɪ]	Ich kann … kaufen.

colours

red	[red]	rot	**brown**	[braʊn]	braun
green	[gri:n]	grün	**white**	[waɪt]	weiß
blue	[blu:]	blau	**orange**	['ɒrɪndʒ]	orange
yellow	['jeləʊ]	gelb	**purple**	['pɜ:pl]	lila; violett
black	[blæk]	schwarz	**pink**	[pɪŋk]	rosa; pink
grey	[greɪ]	grau			

1 Write a dialogue. Schreibe einen Dialog.

Yes. See you later.

Hello, I'm Jonas …

It's time to go …

My name is Elena …

What's your name?

… Nice to meet you.

Jonas: ____________________

____

Elena: ____________________

____

Jonas: ____________________

Bye!

Elena: ____________________

Bye!

2 Write sentences. Schreibe Sätze (über dich selbst).

Hallo! Ich heiße … ____________________

Ich mag (Sport, Tiere, Musik …) ____________________

____

Auf Wiedersehen! ____________________

3 Write what you like. Schreibe auf, was du gerne magst.

1. I like ______________________________ .

2. I like ______________________________ .

3. I like ______________________________ .

4. I like ______________________________ .

5. I like ______________________________ .

4 Write the numbers. Schreibe die Lösungen nicht in Zahlen.

1. one + two = ________________
2. ten – two = ________________
3. three + four = ________________
4. ten : two = ________________
5. two x three = ________________
6. ten – one = ________________
7. four + four = ________________

5 What are the words? Wie heißen die Wörter?

1. ortsp ______________________
2. oeplep ______________________
3. bnemru ______________________
4. kapr ______________________
5. lcoruo ______________________
6. tvitiyac ______________________

6 Choose the right word. Wähle das richtige Wort aus.

1. The dog is in the ______________ (bat/park).
2. He's ______________ (black/blue) and white.
3. And he's ______________ (cool/sport).
4. He and Ben can ______________ (buy/play).
5. Ben: I can buy ______________ (bus/something) here.
6. Ben: And ______________ (tennis/music) is a cool sport here.
7. Ben: I like ______________ (activities/dog) in the park.

7 Find the 11 colours. Finde die elf Farben.

g	b	b	y	m	b	r	p
r	l	t	i	s	r	e	d
e	u	w	b	h	o	g	w
y	e	l	l	o	w	r	w
u	p	s	a	b	n	e	h
f	d	k	c	u	o	e	i
p	i	n	k	p	w	n	t
w	w	p	u	r	p	l	e
g	o	r	a	n	g	e	l

8 What colour? Welche Farbe ist es?

1. red + blue = ______________
2. blue + yellow = ______________
3. yellow + red = ______________
4. black + ______________ = grey
5. red + white = ______________
6. orange + black = ______________

Unit 1 I'm from Greenwich

Way in

p. 12	**I'm from …** ['aɪm ˌfrɒm]	Ich komme aus …
	this [ðɪs]	dies
	my [maɪ]	mein, meine
	bike [baɪk]	Fahrrad
	cool [ku:l]	cool; super
	fan [fæn]	Fan
	eleven [ɪ'levn]	elf
	How old are you? [haʊ‿'əʊld‿ə ˌju:]	Wie alt bist du?
	he's (= he is) [hi:z]	er ist
	crazy ['kreɪzi]	verrückt
p. 13	**England** ['ɪŋglənd]	England
	that's (= that is) [ðæts]	das ist
	Where are you from? [ˌweər‿ə ju 'frɒm]	Woher kommst du?
	pet [pet]	Haustier
	they're (= they are) [ðeə]	sie sind
	guinea pig ['gɪni ˌpɪg]	Meerschweinchen
	twelve [twelv]	zwölf
	lucky number [ˌlʌki 'nʌmbə]	Glückszahl
	cat [kæt]	Katze
p. 12	**photo** ['fəʊtəʊ]	Foto
p. 13	**Germany** ['dʒɜ:məni]	Deutschland

Lerne Vokabeln auch einmal schriftlich: Decke die rechte Spalte ab und übersetze die englischen Wörter ins Deutsche. Versuche ohne Buch, deine deutschen Vokabeln wieder schriftlich ins Englische zu übertragen.

Station 1

family

dad / father [dæd / 'fɑ:ðə]	Papa / Vater	**aunt** [ɑ:nt]	Tante
mum / mother [mʌm / 'mʌðə]	Mama / Mutter	**uncle** ['ʌŋkl]	Onkel
parents *(pl)* ['peərnts]	Eltern	**cousin** ['kʌzn]	Cousin; Cousine
sister ['sɪstə]	Schwester	**grandmother** ['græn,mʌðə]	Großmutter
brother ['brʌðə]	Bruder	**grandfather** ['græn,fɑ:ðə]	Großvater

p. 14	**her** [hɜ:]	ihr, ihre; sie
	family ['fæmli]	Familie
	with [wɪð]	mit
	we're (= we are) [wɪə]	wir sind
	garden ['gɑ:dn]	Garten
	nice [naɪs]	schön; nett
	she's (= she is) [ʃi:z]	sie ist
	next to ['nekst tə]	neben
	me [mi:]	mich; mir
	but [bʌt]	aber
	I have . . . [aɪ 'hæv]	Ich habe . . .
	no [nəʊ]	kein, keine
	me [mi:]	*hier:* ich
	our [aʊə]	unser, unsere
	his [hɪz]	sein, seine
	name [neɪm]	Name
	too [tu:]	auch
	friend [frend]	Freund; Freundin
	of [ɒv]	von
p. 16	**to be** [bi:]	sein
p. 17	**you're (= you are)** [jɔ:]	du bist; ihr seid
	e-mail ['i:meɪl]	E-Mail

personal pronouns

I [aɪ]	ich	**we** [wiː]	wir
you [juː]	du; Sie	**you** [juː]	ihr; Sie
he [hiː]	er	**they** [ðeɪ]	sie *(Pl.)*
she [ʃiː]	sie		
it [ɪt]	es		

Station 2

room things

table ['teɪbl]	Tisch	**bed** [bed]	Bett
shelf *(sg)* [ʃelf], **shelves** *(pl)* [ʃelvz]	Regal; Regalbrett	**wardrobe** ['wɔːdrəʊb]	Kleiderschrank
chair [tʃeə]	Stuhl	**trainer** ['treɪnə]	Turnschuh
box [bɒks]	Box; Kiste	**carpet** ['kɑːpɪt]	Teppich
mobile (phone) ['məʊbaɪl (ˌfəʊn)]	Handy; Mobiltelefon	**scarf** *(sg)* [skɑːf], **scarves** *(pl)* [skɑːvz]	Schal; Tuch
T-shirt ['tiːʃɜːt]	T-Shirt	**lamp** [læmp]	Lampe
poster ['pəʊstə]	Poster	**alarm clock** [ə'lɑːm ˌklɒk]	Wecker
book [bʊk]	Buch; Heft		

p. 18	**bedroom** ['bedrʊm]	Schlafzimmer; Kinderzimmer
	Saturday ['sætədeɪ]	Samstag
	at home [ət 'həʊm]	zu Hause
	Who is it? [ˌhuː 'ɪz‿ɪt]	Wer ist da?
	It's me. [ɪts 'miː]	Ich bin es.
	Are you ready? [ˌɑː juː 'redi]	Bist du fertig?

	under [ˈʌndə]	unter
	late [leɪt]	(zu) spät
	I can't find ... [ˌaɪ kɑːnt ˈfaɪnd]	Ich kann ... nicht finden.
	new [njuː]	neu
	What colour is ...? [ˌwɒt ˈkʌlə ɪz]	Welche Farbe hat ...?
	there's (= there is) [ðeəz]	da ist; dort ist; es gibt
	on [ɒn]	auf; an
	where [weə]	wo; wohin; woher
	there are [ðeər‿ˈɑː]	da sind; es gibt
	your [jɔː]	dein, deine; euer, eure; Ihr, Ihre
	no [nəʊ]	nein
	room [ruːm]	Zimmer; Raum
	mess [mes]	Unordnung; Durcheinander
	what's (= what is) [wɒts]	was ist
p. 19	**right** [raɪt]	richtig; korrekt
	wrong [rɒŋ]	falsch
p. 20	**question** [ˈkwestʃən]	Frage
	favourite [ˈfeɪvrɪt]	Lieblings-
p. 21	**match** [mætʃ]	Spiel
	old [əʊld]	alt
	magazine [ˌmægəˈziːn]	Zeitschrift

Reading corner

p. 22	**tree** [triː]	Baum
	house [haʊs]	Haus
	their [ðeə]	ihr, ihre *(Pl.)*
	big [bɪg]	groß
	wood [wʊd]	Holz
	rope [rəʊp]	Seil
	excited [ɪkˈsaɪtɪd]	aufgeregt; begeistert
	ladder [ˈlædə]	Leiter
	busy [ˈbɪzi]	beschäftigt
	happy [ˈhæpi]	glücklich

What will Holly say? [ˌwɒt wɪl 'hɒli seɪ]	Was wird Holly sagen?
plan [plæn]	Plan
great [greɪt]	großartig; toll
problem ['prɒbləm]	Problem
Thank you. ['θæŋk ju]	Danke.
lunch [lʌnʃ]	Mittagessen
dream [dri:m]	Traum
p. 23 **to sleep** [sli:p]	schlafen
It'll be great fun. [ˌɪtl bɪ 'greɪt fʌn]	Es wird großen Spaß machen.
noise [nɔɪz]	Geräusch
or [ɔ:]	oder
torch [tɔ:tʃ]	Taschenlampe
now [naʊ]	jetzt; nun
sweet [swi:t]	süß
wind [wɪnd]	Wind
song [sɒŋ]	Lied
eye [aɪ]	Auge
night [naɪt]	Nacht

Film corner

rooms

bedroom ['bedrʊm]	Schlafzimmer; Kinderzimmer	**kitchen** ['kɪtʃɪn]	Küche
living room ['lɪvɪŋ ˌrʊm]	Wohnzimmer	**bathroom** ['bɑ:θrʊm]	Bad(ezimmer)

p. 25 **around the house** [ə'raʊnd ðə haʊs]	im Haus
hair straightener ['heə ˌstreɪtnə]	Haarglätter
well [wel]	na ja

	Look ... [lʊk]	Schau mal ...; Schau ... nach.
	thanks [θæŋks]	danke

Listening skills

p. 30	**home** [həʊm]	Zuhause; Heim
p. 31	**dining room** ['daɪnɪŋ ˌrʊm]	Esszimmer
	let's [lets]	lass uns

Manche Wörter kannst du dir als Gegensatzpaare merken:
me ↔ you
right ↔ wrong
black ↔ white

1 Write the family words.

Schreibe die Wörter zum Thema Familie auf.

1. m ________ / m ________ 3. b ________

2. f ________ / d ________ 4. s ________

● 2 Find more family words. Finde mehr Wörter zu Familie.

____

____

3 What's that in English? Was heißt das auf Englisch?

1. seine Schwester ________
2. ihr Bruder ________
3. mein Freund ________
4. unsere Familie ________

4 Write the words. Schreibe die Wörter auf.

1.  ________

2.  ________

3.  ________

4.  ________

5. 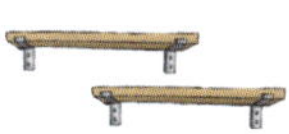 ________

5 Write down the missing letters.

Ergänze die fehlenden Buchstaben.

1. h __ u __ e
2. h __ __ __ y
3. pr __ __ l __ m
4. gr __ __ t
5. __ __ eam
6. ni __ h __
7. bu __ __
8. t __ __ e

6 Where can you find it?

Wo kannst du die Gegenstände finden?

1.  ______________________

2.  ______________________

3. 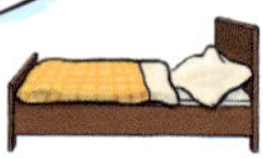 ______________________

4.  ______________________

5.  ______________________

6.  ______________________

7 Draw four pictures. Zeichne vier Bilder.

1. The chair is on the bed.
2. The ball is on the shelf.
3. The cat is under the bed.
4. The books are in the box.

1.	2.
3.	4.

8 Put in the right words. Setze die richtigen Wörter ein.

1.  The book is ____________ the table.
2.  The dog is ____________ the boy.
3.  The mobile is ____________ the chair.
4.  The bike is ____________ the ladder.
5.  The bat is ____________ the box.

● 9 Find seven bedroom words. Write the words in English and German.

Finde sieben Wörter. Schreibe sie auf Englisch und Deutsch auf.

D	B	E	P	L	A	M	P
S	O	X	T	C	F	C	D
N	O	D	M	O	H	K	I
B	K	B	D	M	B	S	S
T	F	X	R	P	N	T	T
I	I	S	H	U	T	C	A
M	B	E	D	T	F	H	B
D	U	R	N	E	D	L	L
W	A	R	D	R	O	B	E
I	T	R	A	I	N	E	R

1. lamp – Lampe; 2. ______________________________

____

____

____

● 10 Write the words.

Schreibe die Wörter auf.

1. onies ______________
2. satpren ______________
3. encul ______________
4. wodo ______________
5. laarm lcokc ______________
6. rladed ______________
7. eter hueso ______________
8. chunl ______________

Unit 2 This is my school

Way in

p. 32	**school** [sku:l]	Schule
	to go [gəʊ]	gehen; fahren
	to [tu:; tʊ; tə]	in; nach; zu
	year [jɪə]	Jahr; Jahrgangsstufe; Klasse
	uniform ['ju:nɪfɔ:m]	Uniform
p. 33	**place** [pleɪs]	Platz; Stelle; Ort
p. 32	**at school** [ət 'sku:l]	in der Schule
p. 33	**playground** ['pleɪgraʊnd]	Schulhof; Pausenhof; Spielplatz
	game [geɪm]	Spiel
	to talk (to) ['tɔ:k tə]	sprechen (mit); reden (mit)
	cafeteria [kæfə'tɪəriə]	Cafeteria; Mensa
	to eat [i:t]	essen
	food [fu:d]	Essen; Nahrung; Lebensmittel
	Mrs ['mɪsɪz]	Frau *(Anrede)*
	caretaker ['keəˌteɪkə]	Hausmeister; Hausmeisterin
	very ['veri]	sehr
	classroom ['klɑ:srʊm]	Klassenzimmer
	tutor group ['tju:tə ˌgru:p]	Klasse *(in einer englischen Schule)*
	tutor ['tju:tə]	Klassenlehrer; Klassenlehrerin
	Mr ['mɪstə]	Herr *(Anrede)*
	Maths [mæθs]	Mathe
	teacher ['ti:tʃə]	Lehrer; Lehrerin
	recording studio [rɪ'kɔ:dɪŋ ˌstju:diəʊ]	Tonstudio
	student ['stju:dnt]	Schüler; Schülerin; Student; Studentin
	to sing [sɪŋ]	singen
p. 32	**I don't like** [aɪ ˌdəʊnt 'laɪk]	ich mag nicht; gefällt mir nicht

Station 1

school things

pen [pen]	Füller; Stift	**calculator** ['kælkjəleɪtə]	(Taschen-) Rechner
exercise book ['eksəsaɪz ˌbʊk]	Übungsheft	**pencil case** ['pensl ˌkeɪs]	Feder-mäppchen
ruler ['ru:lə]	Lineal	**glue** [glu:]	Klebstoff
eraser [ɪ'reɪzə]	Radier-gummi	**felt-tip** [ˌfelt'tɪp]	Filzstift
pencil ['pensl]	Bleistift; Buntstift	**pencil sharpener** ['pensl ˌʃa:pnə]	Anspitzer
bag [bæg]	Tasche		

p. 34	**Wednesday** ['wenzdeɪ]	Mittwoch
	to sit [sɪt]	sitzen
	Don't talk. [ˌdəʊnt 'tɔ:k]	Sei still.; Rede nicht.
	please [pli:z]	bitte
	Close the window. ['kləʊz ðə ˌwɪndəʊ]	Schließe das Fenster.
	Call me ... ['kɔ:l ˌmi]	Nenne mich ...
	good [gʊd]	gut
	singer ['sɪŋə]	Sänger; Sängerin
	to dance [da:ns]	tanzen
	really ['rɪəli]	wirklich
	girl [gɜ:l]	Mädchen
	for [fɔ:]	für
	Sit down. [ˌsɪt 'daʊn]	Setz dich (hin).
	talent show ['tælənt ˌʃəʊ]	Talentwettbewerb
	next [nekst]	nächste/-r/-s
	week [wi:k]	Woche
	to take out [ˌteɪk‿'aʊt]	herausnehmen
	to open ['əʊpn]	öffnen; aufmachen
	to look at ['lʊk‿ət]	anschauen
	board [bɔ:d]	Tafel

	to **do** [du:]	machen; tun
	Put your hands up. ['pʊt jɔ: ˌhændz‿ʌp]	Meldet euch.
	an [ən]	ein, eine
p. 35	**Sorry about ...** ['sɒri ˌəbaʊt]	Es tut mir leid wegen ...
	Here you are. [ˌhɪə ju‿'ɑ:]	Bitte schön.
	Excuse me. [ɪk'skju:z mi]	Entschuldigung!
	to **help** [help]	helfen
	toilet ['tɔɪlət]	Toilette
	to **write** [raɪt]	schreiben
	to **say** [seɪ]	sagen; sprechen
	of course [əv 'kɔ:s]	natürlich; selbstverständlich
	sure [ʃʊə]	sicher
	Sorry. ['sɒri]	Tut mir leid.; Entschuldigung.
p. 36	**page** [peɪdʒ]	Seite
	workbook ['wɜ:kbʊk]	Arbeitsheft
	class [klɑ:s]	Unterricht
	to **listen (to)** ['lɪsn]	zuhören; anhören; hören
	to **forget** [fə'get]	vergessen
	exercise ['eksəsaɪz]	Übung
p. 37	to **put** [pʊt]	setzen; legen; stellen

Du kannst dir ein Wort besser merken, wenn du es in deinem Kopf mit einem Bild verbindest.

Station 2

days

Monday ['mʌndeɪ] **(Mon)**	Montag
Tuesday ['tju:zdeɪ] **(Tues)**	Dienstag
Wednesday ['wenzdeɪ] **(Wed)**	Mittwoch
Thursday ['θɜ:zdeɪ] **(Thurs)**	Donnerstag
Friday ['fraɪdeɪ] **(Fri)**	Freitag
Saturday ['sætədeɪ] **(Sat)**	Samstag
Sunday ['sʌndeɪ] **(Sun)**	Sonntag

school subjects

(DT) [ˌdi:'ti:] **Design Technology** [dɪˌzaɪn tek'nɒlədʒi]	Technik
PE [ˌpi:'i:] **(Physical Education)** [ˌfɪzɪkl edʒʊ'keɪʃn]	Sportunterricht
Maths [mæθs]	Mathe
French [frentʃ]	Französisch
Art [ɑ:t]	Kunst
Science [saɪəns]	Wissenschaft; Naturwissenschaft
English ['ɪŋglɪʃ]	Englisch
Music ['mju:zɪk]	Musik
German ['dʒɜ:mən]	Deutsch
RE [ˌɑ:‿'ri:] **(Religious Education)** [rɪˌlɪdʒəs‿edʒʊ'keɪʃn]	Religionsunterricht
IT [ˌaɪ'ti:] **(Information Technology)** [ɪnfəˌmeɪʃn tek'nɒlədʒi]	Informatik; Informationstechnik
History ['hɪstri]	Geschichte

Geography [dʒi'ɒgrəfi]	Geografie; Erdkunde
Biology [baɪ'ɒlədʒi]	Biologie
Social Studies ['səʊʃl ˌstʌdiz]	Gesellschaftslehre; Sozialkunde

p. 38	**at break** [ət 'breɪk]	in der Pause
	lesson ['lesn]	Schulstunde; Unterricht
	Ms [mɪz]	Frau *(Anrede)*
	timetable ['taɪmˌteɪbl]	Stundenplan
	subject ['sʌbdʒɪkt]	Schulfach
	easy ['i:zi]	einfach; leicht
	You're right. [jɔ:‿'raɪt]	Du hast Recht.
	to be good at [bi 'gʊd‿ət]	gut sein in/bei
	spelling ['spelɪŋ]	Rechtschreibung
	joke [dʒəʊk]	Witz
	funny ['fʌni]	lustig; witzig
	interesting ['ɪntrəstɪŋ]	interessant
	on Tuesday [ˌɒn 'tju:zdeɪ]	am Dienstag; dienstags
	day [deɪ]	Tag
	to spell [spel]	buchstabieren
	like [laɪk]	wie
	yours [jɔ:z]	deine; eure; Ihre
	registration [ˌredʒɪ'streɪʃn]	Überprüfung der Anwesenheit
p. 39	**boring** ['bɔ:rɪŋ]	langweilig
	fun [fʌn]	Freude; Spaß
	difficult ['dɪfɪklt]	schwierig
	alphabet ['ælfəbet]	Alphabet

the alphabet

a [eɪ]	**g** [dʒi:]	**m** [em]	**s** [es]	**x** [eks]
b [bi:]	**h** [eɪtʃ]	**n** [en]	**t** [ti:]	**y** [waɪ]
c [si:]	**i** [ai]	**o** [əʊ]	**u** [ju:]	**z** [zed]
d [di:]	**j** [dʒeɪ]	**p** [pi:]	**v** [vi:]	
e [i:]	**k** [keɪ]	**q** [kju:]	**w** ['dʌbl ju:]	
f [ef]	**l** [el]	**r** [a:]		

Reading corner

p. 42	**trick** [trɪk]	Trick; Streich
	saxophone ['sæksəfəʊn]	Saxophon
	lunch [lʌnʃ]	Mittagessen
	talent ['tælənt]	Talent
	winner ['wɪnə]	Sieger; Siegerin; Gewinner; Gewinnerin
p. 43	**later** ['leɪtə]	später
	Well done! [ˌwel 'dʌn]	Gut gemacht!
	star [stɑː]	Star
	all [ɔːl]	alle
	uncle ['ʌŋkl]	Onkel
	Indian ['ɪndiən]	indisch
	restaurant ['restrɒnt]	Restaurant
	What a … ['wɒt‿ə]	Was für ein/eine …

Film corner

p. 45	to **make friends** [ˌmeɪk 'frendz]	Freundschaften schließen
	to **make** [meɪk]	machen; tun; bilden
	chewing gum ['tʃuːɪŋ ˌgʌm]	Kaugummi
	jeans *(pl)* [dʒiːnz]	Jeans
	Alicia put it in there. [ə'lɪʃə pʊt‿ɪt ˌɪn ˌðeə]	Alicia hat es dort hinein getan.
	film [fɪlm]	Film

Falls du das Workbook zu Orange Line 1 mit Lernsoftware hast, kannst du deine Aussprache damit gezielt üben: Die Wörter werden vorgesprochen. Versuche sie so genau wie möglich nachzusprechen und nimm dich mit dem Mikro auf.

1 Find the words and make sentences with can.

Finde die Verben und bilde Sätze mit can.

naced • kalt • og • isgn • tea • poen

1. I can ______________________ in the cafeteria.
2. I ______________________ to school.
3. I ______________________ the window.
4. I ______________________ my favourite song.
5. I ______________________ in my room.
6. I ______________________ to Mrs Preston.

2 School: Find and write the words.

Schule: Finde die Wörter.

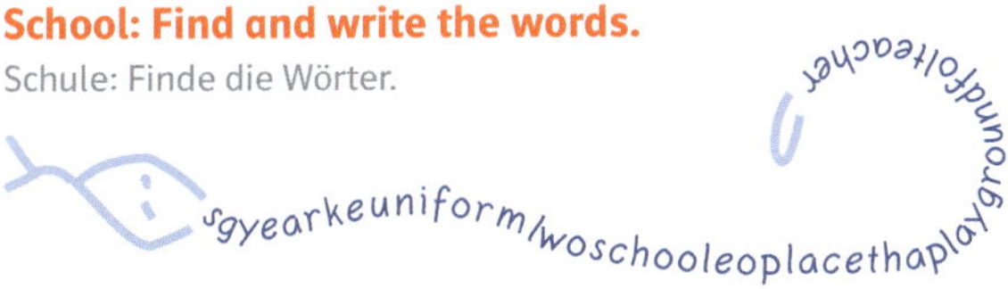

a) Write the words.
Schreibe die Wörter auf.

b) What is it in German?
Wie heißt es auf Deutsch?

1. ______________________ ______________________
2. ______________________ ______________________
3. ______________________ ______________________
4. ______________________ ______________________
5. ______________________ ______________________
6. ______________________ ______________________

3 Write the words. Schreibe die Wörter auf.

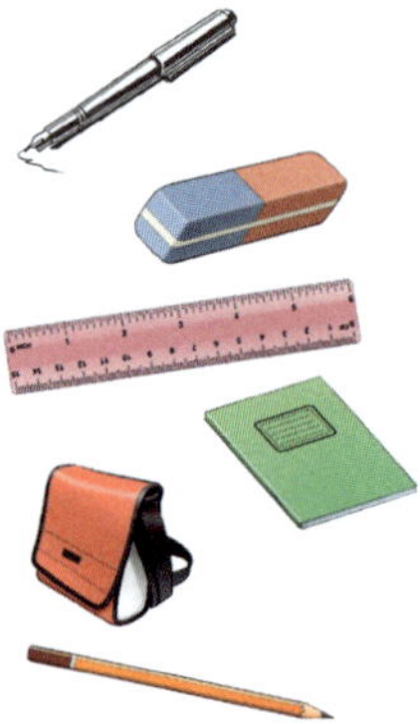

1. ______________________
2. ______________________
3. ______________________
4. ______________________
5. ______________________
6. ______________________

4 What's the word? Setze das richtige Wort ein.

1. In my bag there is a ______________________ (caretaker/red pencil).
2. I can ______________ (read/write) with a pen.
3. In my bag there is ______________________ (an eraser/a window).
4. You can ______________ (close/sit) on a chair.
5. Teacher: ______________ (open/dance) your books.
6. I can write the answer in my ______________________ (ruler/exercise book).

5 Complete the words. Vervollständige die Wörter.

1. w__ __k
2. s__ __g__ __
3. __ __ass__ __ __m
4. v__ __ __
5. w__ __ __o__
6. ta__ __nt __ __ __w
7. p__ __ __s__
8. r__ __ __ __y
9. re__ __ __ __ __ __ __ s__ __dio
10. tu__ __r

6 Write the words and find the pairs.

Schreibe die Wörter auf, dann finde die Paare.

1.  ____________________ finger

2.  ____________________ girl

3.  ____________________ answer

4.  ____________________ song

5.  ____________________ close

6.  ____________________ student

7 Write a or an. Schreibe a oder an.

1. ______ animal
2. ______ tree
3. ______ exercise book
4. ______ board
5. ______ boy
6. ______ window
7. ______ activity
8. ______ eraser
9. ______ girl
10. ______ Art lesson

8 Put in the right verbs. Setze die richtigen Verben ein.

1. I can ________________ the saxophone in my room.
2. You can ________________ to Mrs Preston.
3. Please ________________ next to me.
4. Can we ________________ to music in the classroom?
5. Yes, you can ________________ the exercise. It's easy!
6. Listen and ________________ the words.
7. Now ________________ the words in your exercise book.
8. You can ________________ at the board.

9 Complete Luke's sentences. Vervollständige Lukes Sätze.

School timetable

	Mon	Tue	Wed	Thu	Fri
Lesson 1	Maths	Art	Science	Design Technology	German
Lesson 2	French	German	Science	Art	Physical Education

1. On ______________ I have Art and ______________ ______________ .
2. I have German on ______________ and ______________ .
3. On ______________ I have ______________ and French.
4. And on ______________ I have Science.

10 And Tom? Vervollständige Toms Sätze.

1. Tom's favourite subject is  ______________ .
2. He has  ______________ on Tuesday and Friday.
3.  ______________ is interesting.
4. He has no school on ______________ and ______________ .
5.  ______________ isn't his favourite subject.

11 Find the words and write them.

Finde die Wörter und schreibe sie auf.

1. itemltaeb ______________________________
2. usjbetc ______________________________
3. pllesngi ______________________________
4. plahateb ______________________________
5. koje ______________________________
6. selson ______________________________

12 What's that in German/English?

Wie sagst du das auf Deutsch/Englisch?

1. Du hast Recht. ______________________________ .
2. I'm good at French. ______________________________
______________________________ .
3. You make friends. ______________________________
______________________________ .
4. Ich mag Kaugummi. ______________________________ .
5. Kannst du das bitte buchstabieren? ______________________________
______________________________ ?

●13 What's wrong here?

Unterstreiche die Wörter, die hier nicht passen, und schreibe sie auf Deutsch auf.

1. History – boring – Geography ______________________
2. winner – felt-tip – pencil sharpener ______________________
3. saxophone – Science – Maths ______________________
4. star – music – restaurant ______________________
5. sing – dance – difficult ______________________

●14 School things or school subjects?

Schreibe die Wörter in die jeweils richtige Box.

Information Technology • felt-tip • Geography • RE • calculator • Maths • pencil case • glue • History • PE • pen

School things	School subjects
______________________	______________________
______________________	______________________
______________________	______________________
______________________	______________________
______________________	______________________
	______________________

Unit 3 My free time

Way in

p. 52	**free time** [ˌfri: ˈtaɪm]	Freizeit
	after [ˈɑ:ftə]	nach
	on Wednesdays [ɒn ˈwenzdeɪz]	mittwochs
	to watch TV [ˌwɒtʃ ti:ˈvi:]	fernsehen
	to love [lʌv]	lieben; gern mögen
	programme [ˈprəʊgræm]	Programm; Sendung
	to want (to) [wɒnt (tə)]	wollen
	famous [ˈfeɪməs]	berühmt
	netball [ˈnetbɔ:l]	Korbball
	team [ti:m]	Team; Mannschaft
	to win [wɪn]	gewinnen; siegen
	a lot [ə ˈlɒt]	viel
p. 53	**practice** [ˈpræktɪs]	Training; Übung
	at [æt]	an; in; um; bei; auf
	lunchtime [ˈlʌnʃtaɪm]	Mittagszeit; Mittagspause
	to run [rʌn]	rennen; laufen
	around [əˈraʊnd]	herum; umher
	then [ðen]	dann; danach
	captain [ˈkæptɪn]	Kapitän; Kapitänin
	at the weekend [ˌət ðə ˈwi:kend]	am Wochenende
	cinema [ˈsɪnəmə]	Kino
	movie [ˈmu:vi]	Film
	every [ˈevri]	jeder
	month [mʌnθ]	Monat
	science fiction [ˌsaɪəns ˈfɪkʃn]	Science-Fiction
	animal rescue shelter [ˌænɪml ˈreskju: ˌʃeltə]	Tierheim

Station 1

animals

horse [hɔ:s]	Pferd	**mouse** *(sg)* [maʊs], **mice** *(pl)* [maɪs]	Maus
monkey ['mʌŋki]	Affe	**bird** [bɜ:d]	Vogel
bear [beə]	Bär	**fish** *(sg)* [fɪʃ], **fish** *(pl)* [fɪʃ]	Fisch
tiger ['taɪgə]	Tiger	**lion** ['laɪən]	Löwe
elephant ['elɪfənt]	Elefant	**flamingo** [flə'mɪŋgəʊ]	Flamingo
snake [sneɪk]	Schlange	**zebra** ['zebrə]	Zebra
parrot ['pærət]	Papagei	**crocodile** ['krɒkədaɪl]	Krokodil
giraffe [dʒɪ'rɑ:f]	Giraffe	**camel** ['kæml]	Kamel
penguin ['peŋgwɪn]	Pinguin		

Mit einem Partner oder einer Partnerin lernen sich Vokabeln leichter:
Fragt euch gegenseitig ab.
A: Vogel? B: Bird!

numbers 11 – 100

eleven 11 [ɪ'levn]	elf
twelve 12 [twelv]	zwölf
thirteen 13 [θɜː'tiːn]	dreizehn
fourteen 14 [ˌfɔː'tiːn]	vierzehn
fifteen 15 [ˌfɪf'tiːn]	fünfzehn
sixteen 16 [ˌsɪk'stiːn]	sechzehn
seventeen 17 [ˌsevn'tiːn]	siebzehn
eighteen 18 [ˌeɪ'tiːn]	achtzehn
nineteen 19 [ˌnaɪn'tiːn]	neunzehn
twenty 20 ['twenti]	zwanzig
twenty-one 21 ['twentiˌwʌn]	einundzwanzig
twenty-two 22 ['twentiˌtuː]	zweiundzwanzig
thirty 30 ['θɜːti]	dreißig
forty 40 ['fɔːti]	vierzig
fifty 50 ['fɪfti]	fünfzig
sixty 60 ['sɪksti]	sechzig
seventy 70 ['sevnti]	siebzig
eighty 80 ['eɪti]	achtzig
ninety 90 ['naɪnti]	neunzig
a/one hundred 100 ['hʌndrəd]	einhundert

p. 54	**zoo** [zuː]	Zoo; Tierpark
	to come [kʌm]	kommen
	India ['ɪndiə]	Indien
	years old [ˌjɪəz‿'əʊld]	Jahre alt
	metre ['miːtə]	Meter
	high [haɪ]	hoch; groß
	to walk [wɔːk]	gehen
	fruit [fruːt]	Frucht; Obst
	also ['ɔːlsəʊ]	auch

	grass [grɑːs]	Gras
	much [mʌtʃ]	viel
	only ['əʊnli]	nur
	four hours a day [ˌaʊəz‿ə 'deɪ]	vier Stunden täglich
	age [eɪdʒ]	Alter
	meat [miːt]	Fleisch
	7 kilograms a day [ˌkɪləgræmz‿ə 'deɪ]	sieben Kilogramm täglich
	other ['ʌðə]	andere; weitere
	information *(no pl)* [ˌɪnfə'meɪʃn]	Information; Informationen
	centimetre (cm) ['sentɪˌmiːtə]	Zentimeter (cm)
	40 kilometres an hour [kɪ'lɒmɪtəz‿ən‿'aʊə]	40 Kilometer pro Stunde
	small [smɔːl]	klein
	plant [plɑːnt]	Pflanze
	long [lɒŋ]	lang
	for five months [fə 'faɪv ˌmʌnθs]	fünf Monate lang
	winter ['wɪntə]	Winter
p. 55	**to work** [wɜːk]	arbeiten
	zookeeper [ˌzuː'kiːpə]	Tierpfleger; Tierpflegerin
p. 56	**What about ...?** ['wɒt‿əˌbaʊt]	Was ist mit ...?
	banana [bə'nɑːnə]	Banane
	lots of ['lɒts‿əv]	viel; jede Menge

Wenn du Wörter oder Redewendungen schwierig findest, schreibe sie auf und markiere die Schwierigkeiten deutlich mit Farbe, z.B. fourteen – forty.

Station 2

daily routines

get up [ˌgetˬˈʌp]	aufstehen	**have breakfast** [ˌhæv ˈbrekfəst]	frühstücken
eat … [iːt]	… essen	**have lunch** [ˌhaev ˈlʌnʃ]	zu Mittag essen
go … [gəʊ]	… gehen	**go to bed** [ˌgəʊ tə ˈbed]	ins Bett gehen
walk … [wɔːk]	… gehen	**call** [kɔːl]	rufen; anrufen
feed … [fiːd]	… füttern		
play … [pleɪ]	… spielen		
sleep [sliːp]	schlafen		
clean … [kliːn]	… sauber machen; … putzen		

p. 58	**a busy day** [ə ˌbɪzi ˈdeɪ]	ein ausgefüllter Tag
	to interview [ˈɪntəvjuː]	interviewen; befragen
	when [wen]	wann
	o'clock [əˈklɒk]	Uhr *(Zeitangabe bei vollen Stunden)*
	why [waɪ]	warum
	early [ˈɜːli]	früh
	breakfast [ˈbrekfəst]	Frühstück
	first [fɜːst]	zuerst; als Erstes
	cage [keɪdʒ]	Käfig
	after that [ˈɑːftə ðət]	danach
	in the afternoon [ˌɪn ði ˌɑːftəˈnuːn]	nachmittags
	dirty [ˈdɜːti]	dreckig; schmutzig
	work [wɜːk]	Arbeit
	What time is it? [ˌwɒt ˈtaɪmˬɪzˬɪt]	Wie spät ist es?; Wie viel Uhr ist es?
p. 59	**half past (two)** [ˌhɑːf ˈpɑːst]	halb (drei)
	oh [əʊ]	null *(bei Uhrzeiten und Telefonnummern)*
	past [pɑːst]	nach *(bei Uhrzeitangaben)*

	quarter past ['kwɔ:tə pɑ:st]	Viertel nach
	quarter to ['kwɔ:tə tə]	Viertel vor
	to [tu:; tʊ; tə]	vor *(bei Uhrzeitangaben)*
	tea [ti:]	Tee; (frühes) Abendessen
p. 60	**shopping** ['ʃɒpɪŋ]	Einkaufen
p. 61	**home** [həʊm]	nach Hause

Reading corner

p. 62	**café** ['kæfeɪ]	Café
	mystery ['mɪstri]	Rätsel; Geheimnis
	story ['stɔ:ri]	Geschichte
	with his trainers on [ˌwɪð hɪz 'treɪnəz‿ɒn]	und hat Turnschuhe an
	lead [li:d]	Leine
	to **fall** [fɔ:l]	fallen
	floor [flɔ:]	Fußboden
	clever ['klevə]	schlau; klug; intelligent
	a lot of [ə 'lɒt‿əv]	viel(e); eine Menge
	hungry ['hʌŋgri]	hungrig
	woman *(sg)* ['wʊmən], **women** *(pl)* ['wɪmɪn]	Frau
	police officer [pə'li:s‿ɒfɪsə]	Polizeibeamter; Polizeibeamtin
	upset [ʌp'set]	aufgebracht; bestürzt
	all over [ˌɔ:l‿'əʊvə]	überall
	we'll (= we will) [wi:l]	wir werden
	burglar ['bɜ:glə]	Einbrecher; Einbrecherin
	There's no money missing. [ðeəz nəʊ 'mʌni mɪsɪŋ]	Es fehlt kein Geld.
	No idea! [ˌnəʊ‿aɪ'dɪə]	Keine Ahnung!
	to **lock** [lɒk]	abschließen
	how [haʊ]	wie
	to **get in** ['get‿ɪn]	hereinkommen
	maybe ['meɪbi]	vielleicht
	to **solve** [sɒlv]	lösen
	nose [nəʊz]	Nase

	clue [klu:]	Hinweis; Spur
	wool [wʊl]	Wolle
	nut [nʌt]	Nuss
	hole [həʊl]	Loch
	ceiling ['si:lɪŋ]	Zimmerdecke
	Who's up there? [ˌhuz ʌp 'ðeə]	Wer ist da oben?
	raccoon [rə'ku:n]	Waschbär
p. 63	**Dear …,** [dɪə]	Liebe/Lieber … *(Anrede in Briefen)*
	help [help]	Hilfe
	drink [drɪŋk]	Getränk
	Yours, [jɔ:z]	Eure *(als Briefabschluss)*

Film corner

p. 65	**the fastest** [ðə 'fa:stɪst]	der/die/das schnellste

Spiele „I spy …" mit einem Partner oder einer Partnerin, damit du dir die neuen Wörter besser einprägen kannst:

A: I spy with my little eye something on page 63 (in our English book). It's black and white.
B: Is it Sherlock?
A: No, that's wrong.
B: Is it the raccoon?
A: Yes, that's right.

1 Complete the sentences. Vervollständige die Sätze.

free time | team | cinema | every
netball | run | watch | football practice

1. On Wednesdays I go to the ______________________ .
2. After school I play ______________________ .
3. I help my family in my ______________________ .
4. At the weekend I go to ______________________ .
5. There I help my ______________________ .
6. On Sundays I ______________________ TV.
7. ______________ day I ______________ in the park.

2 Complete the words and write the German word.

Vervollständige die Wörter und schreibe sie auf Deutsch auf.

1. ca_ _ai_ ______________________
2. f_ _ _us ______________________
3. _ro_ nd ______________________
4. pro_ _a_ _e ______________________
5. lu_c_ _ _m_ ______________________
6. a_ _ _r ______________________

3 Find and write the words.

Finde die Wörter und schreibe sie auf.

triwatchTVhliihelpfdiolovetfbirunlheiwinalfiwantcocomefg

1. watch TV fernsehen
2.
3.
4.
5.
6.
7.

4 Words for pictures. Finde die Wörter für die Bilder.

1. 
2. 
3. 
4. 
5. 
6. 

5 Write the number after the word.

Schreibe die Zahlen auf.

twenty-four	______	twenty-nine	______
eighty-eight	______	fifty-eight	______
thirty	______	one hundred	______
sixty-three	______	twelve	______

6 Write the numbers in words.

Schreibe die Lösungen nicht in Zahlen.

1. eight + eight = ______
2. nineteen + six = ______
3. fifteen – three = ______
4. thirty + thirty + thirty = ______
5. ten + ten = ______
6. thirty – thirteen = ______
7. sixty-one + thirty-eight = ______
8. a hundred – sixty = ______

7 What's their food? Was fressen sie?

a) Write the words. Schreibe die Wörter.

1.

ssrga

____

2.

nbaaans

____

3.

team

____

4.

tuifr

____

5.

cemi

____

6.

stplan

____

b) Complete the sentences with the right word from a).
Ergänze die Sätze mit den richtigen Wörtern aus a).

1. A horse eats grass ______________.
2. A monkey eats ______________.
3. A tiger eats ______________.
4. A p______________.
5. A s______________.
6. An e______________.

8 Fred's day: Complete the sentences.

Ergänze die Sätze über Freds Tag.

1. Der Tierpfleger steht auf.	The ______________________ .
2. Er isst eine Banane zum Frühstück.	He eats ______________________ for ______________________ .
3. Er geht zum Zoo.	He __________ to the __________ .
4. Zuerst füttert er die Pinguine.	__________ he feeds the ______________________ .
5. Danach spielt er mit den Affen.	__________ he __________ with ______________________ .
6. Ihre Käfige sind schmutzig.	Their __________ are __________ .
7. Er putzt ihre Käfige.	He __________ their __________ .
8. Er liebt seine Arbeit.	He __________ his work.
9. Er ist neun Stunden am Tag im Zoo.	He is in the zoo for ______________________ .

9 What are the words? Wie heißen die Wörter?

a) Find the words. (→↓) Finde die Wörter. (→↓)

G	M	E	A	T	L	O	W	H	Y
S	A	F	T	E	R	N	O	O	N
M	G	T	E	U	P	L	R	W	E
A	A	L	S	O	I	Y	K	K	A
L	Z	G	F	S	T	O	R	Y	G
L	I	M	Y	S	T	E	R	Y	E
I	N	T	E	R	V	I	E	W	F
V	E	F	A	N	T	L	O	N	G
B	H	A	U	P	M	E	T	V	H

b) Write the words down in English and German.
Schreibe die Wörter auf Englisch und Deutsch auf.

→ 1. meat – Fleisch
2. w
3. a
4. a
5. s
6. m
7. i
8. l

↓ 9. s
10. m
11. o
12. w
13. h
14. a

10 What time is it? Wie spät ist es?

Draw the time. Zeichne die Zeiten in die Uhren ein.

1. It's half past ten.

2. It's a quarter past four.

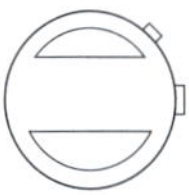

3. It's seven forty-five.

4. It's ten to nine.

● 11 Write the time in words. Schreibe die Uhrzeit in Worten.

1. 

It's *one fifteen* ____________________.

2. 

It's ______________________________.

3. 

________________________ in the morning.

4. 

____

or ________________________.

5. 

__________________________________ or

____________________________________.

Unit 4 Let's celebrate!

Way in

months

January ['dʒænjuri]	Januar	**August** ['ɔ:gəst]	August
February ['februri]	Februar	**September** [sep'tembə]	September
March [mɑ:tʃ]	März	**October** [ɒk'təʊbə]	Oktober
April ['eɪprl]	April	**November** [nə'vembə]	November
May [meɪ]	Mai	**December** [dɪ'sembə]	Dezember
June [dʒu:n]	Juni		
July [dʒʊ'laɪ]	Juli		

p. 70	**to celebrate** ['seləbreɪt]	feiern
p. 71	**Trick or treat!** [ˌtrɪk‿ə 'tri:t]	Süßes, sonst gibt's Saures!
p. 70	**in August** [in 'ɔ:gəst]	im August
	special ['speʃl]	besonders; speziell
	to wear [weə]	tragen *(Kleidung)*
	scary ['skeəri]	gruselig; beängstigend
	costume ['kɒstju:m]	Kostüm
	to collect [kə'lekt]	sammeln
	money ['mʌni]	Geld
	evening ['i:vnɪŋ]	Abend
	fire [faɪə]	Feuer
	Eid [i:d]	Eid *(muslimisches Fest)*
	Muslim ['mʊzlɪm]	Muslim; Muslimin
	different ['dɪfrnt]	anders; unterschiedlich
	together [tə'geðə]	zusammen; gemeinsam
	to get [get]	bekommen
	clothes *(pl)* [kləʊðz]	Kleider *(Pl.)*; Kleidung
	sweet [swi:t]	Süßigkeit; Bonbon

p. 71 **birthday** ['bɜ:θdeɪ] Geburtstag
party ['pɑ:ti] Party; Feier
Christmas ['krɪsməs] Weihnachten

Station 1

ordinal numbers

first (1st) [fɜ:st]	erste
second (2nd) ['seknd]	zweite
third (3rd) [θɜ:d]	dritte
fourth (4th) [fɔ:θ]	vierte
fifth (5th) [fɪfθ]	fünfte
sixth (6th) [sɪkθ]	sechste
seventh (7th) ['sevnθ]	siebte
eighth (8th) [eɪtθ]	achte
ninth (9th) [naɪnθ]	neunte
tenth (10th) [tenθ]	zehnte
eleventh (11th) [ɪ'levnθ]	elfte
twelfth (12th) [twelfθ]	zwölfte
thirteenth (13th) [ˌθɜ:'ti:nθ]	dreizehnte
fourteenth (14th) [ˌfɔ:'ti:nθ]	vierzehnte
fifteenth (15th) [ˌfɪf'ti:nθ]	fünfzehnte
sixteenth (16th) [ˌsɪk'sti:nθ]	sechzehnte

seventeenth (17th) [ˌsevnˈtiːnθ]	siebzehnte
eighteenth (18th) [ˌeɪˈtiːnθ]	achtzehnte
nineteenth (19th) [ˌnaɪnˈtiːnθ]	neunzehnte
twentieth (20th) [ˈtwentiəθ]	zwanzigste
21st [ˌtwentiˈfɜːst]	einundzwanzigste
22nd [ˌtwentiˈseknd]	zweiundzwanzigste
23rd [ˌtwentiˈθɜːd]	dreiundzwanzigste
24th [ˌtwentiˈfɔːθ]	vierundzwanzigste
25th [ˌtwentiˈfɪfθ]	fünfundzwanzigste
26th [ˌtwentiˈsɪkθ]	sechsundzwanzigste
27th [ˌtwentiˈsevnθ]	siebenundzwanzigste
28th [ˌtwentiˈeɪtθ]	achtundzwanzigste
29th [ˌtwentiˈnaɪnθ]	neunundzwanzigste
thirtieth (30th) [ˈθɜːtiəθ]	dreißigste
fortieth (40th) [ˈfɔːtiəθ]	vierzigste
fiftieth (50th) [ˈfɪftiəθ]	fünfzigste
sixtieth (60th) [ˈsɪkstiəθ]	sechzigste
seventieth (70th) [ˈsevntiəθ]	siebzigste
eightieth (80th) [ˈeɪtiəθ]	achtzigste
ninetieth (90th) [ˈnaɪntiəθ]	neunzigste
hundredth (100th) [ˈhʌndrədθ]	hundertste

birthday activities

to **have a fancy dress party** [ˌfænsi ˈdres]	eine Verkleidungsparty machen
to **have a barbecue party** [ˈbɑ:bɪkju:]	eine Grillparty machen
to **invite my friends** [ɪnˈvaɪt]	meine Freunde einladen
to **go to the cinema** [ˈsɪnəmə]	ins Kino gehen
to **watch movies** [ˈmu:vi:z]	Filme schauen
to **have a picnic in the park** [ˈpɪknɪk]	ein Picknick im Park machen
to **have a sleepover** [ˈsli:pˌəʊvə]	eine Übernachtungsparty machen
to **go to a theme park** [ˈθi:m ˌpɑ:k]	in einen Freizeitpark gehen
to **go to a fast food restaurant** [ˌfɑ:st fu:d ˈrestrɒnt]	in ein Fastfood-Restaurant gehen
to **have a favourite meal** [ˈfeɪvrɪt ˌmi:l]	ein Lieblingsessen genießen

p. 72	**present** [ˈpreznt]	Geschenk
	him [hɪm]	ihm; ihn
	surprise [səˈpraɪz]	Überraschung
	on 7th July [ɒn ðə ˈsevnθ əv ˌdʒʊlaɪ]	am 7. Juli
	always [ˈɔ:lweɪz]	immer
	to **make a cake** [ˌmeɪk‿ə ˈkeɪk]	einen Kuchen backen
	chocolate [ˈtʃɒklət]	Schokolade
	to **give** [gɪv]	geben
	card [kɑ:d]	Karte; Spielkarte
	cute [kju:t]	niedlich; süß
	never [ˈnevə]	nie; niemals
	often [ˈɒfn]	oft; häufig
	sometimes [ˈsʌmtaɪmz]	manchmal
	not [nɒt]	nicht

	bad [bæd]	schlecht
	is more fun [ɪz 'mɔː ˌfʌn]	macht mehr Spaß
	more [mɔː]	mehr
	fun [fʌn]	Spaß; Freude
p. 73	**date** [deɪt]	Datum
	like this [laɪk 'ðɪs]	so; auf diese Weise
	burger ['bɜːgə]	Hamburger
	ice cream [ˌaɪs 'kriːm]	Eiscreme; Eis
	strawberry ['strɔːbri]	Erdbeere
p. 75	**to know** [nəʊ]	wissen; kennen

Station 2

food

coke [kəʊk]	Cola	**sandwich** ['sænwɪdʒ]	Sandwich; belegtes Brot
crisp [krɪsp]	Kartoffelchip	**cake** [keɪk]	Kuchen
butter ['bʌtə]	Butter	**peach** [piːtʃ]	Pfirsich
milk [mɪlk]	Milch	**biscuit** ['bɪskɪt]	Keks
chocolate ['tʃɒklət]	Schokolade	**flour** [flaʊə]	Mehl
egg [eg]	Ei	**lemonade** [ˌlemə'neɪd]	Limonade
sugar ['ʃʊgə]	Zucker	**pasta** ['pæstə]	Pasta; Nudeln
orange ['ɒrɪndʒ]	Orange		
cheese [tʃiːz]	Käse		

p. 76	**Let's see …** [ˌlets 'siː]	Lass mal sehen …; Also …
	balloon [bə'luːn]	Luftballon
	bar of chocolate [bɑːr‿əv 'tʃɒklət]	Tafel Schokolade
	candle ['kændl]	Kerze
	corner shop ['kɔːnə ˌʃɒp]	Tante-Emma-Laden
	shop [ʃɒp]	Laden; Geschäft

	How can I help you? [ˌhaʊ kæn aɪ ˈhelp‿ju]	Was kann ich für dich tun?
	to need [ni:d]	brauchen
	some [sʌm]	einige; ein paar
	thing [θɪŋ]	Sache; Ding
	box [bɒks]	Schachtel
	Anything else? [ˈeniθɪŋ ˌels]	Darf es sonst noch etwas sein?
	packet [ˈpækɪt]	Packung; Tüte
	How much (is/are) ...? [ˌhaʊ ˈmʌtʃ‿ɪz/ɑ:]	Wie viel (kostet/kosten) ...?
	... are 99p. [ɑ: ˈnaɪntinaɪn ˌpens]	... kosten 99 Pence.
	... is £1.25. [ɪz ˈwʌn paʊnd twentiˌfaɪv]	... kostet ein Pfund fünfundzwanzig.
	so [səʊ]	deshalb; also
	That's £2.24. [ðæts ˈtu: paʊndz ˌtwenti fɔ:]	Das macht zwei Pfund und 24 Pence.
	You're welcome. [jɔ: ˈwelkəm]	Gern geschehen.
	Here's your change. [ˌhɪəz jɔ: ˈtʃeɪndʒ]	Hier ist dein Wechselgeld.
p. 77	**bottle** [ˈbɒtl]	Flasche
	can [kæn]	Dose
p. 78	**I'm sorry.** [aɪm ˈsɒrɪ]	Es tut mir leid.; Entschuldigung.
	CD [ˌsi:ˈdi:]	CD
p. 79	**to read** [ri:d]	lesen
	DVD [ˌdi:vi:ˈdi:]	DVD
	shopping list [ˈʃɒpɪŋ ˌlɪst]	Einkaufszettel
	Pardon? [ˈpɑ:dn]	Wie bitte?

Reading corner

p. 80	**witch** [wɪtʃ]	Hexe
	superman [ˈsu:pəmæn]	Superman
	carnival [ˈkɑ:nɪvl]	Karneval; Fasching

	dancer ['dɑ:nsə]	Tänzer; Tänzerin
	smurf [smɜ:f]	Schlumpf
	alien ['eɪliən]	Außerirdischer; Außerirdische
	narrator [nə'reɪtə]	Erzähler; Erzählerin
	invitation [ˌɪnvɪ'teɪʃn]	Einladung
	Happy birthday! [ˌhæpi 'bɜ:θdeɪ]	Alles Gute zum Geburtstag!
	the others [ði‿'ʌðəz]	die anderen
	everyone ['evriwʌn]	jeder
	Be careful! [ˌbi: 'keəfl]	Sei vorsichtig!
	to **be scared** [bi 'skeəd]	Angst haben
	I don't know! [ˌaɪ ˌdəʊnt 'nəʊ]	Ich weiß (es) nicht!
	to **think** [θɪŋk]	denken; glauben
	pirate ['paɪrət]	Seeräuber; Seeräuberin; Pirat; Piratin
p. 81	**dance** [dɑ:ns]	Tanz
	Look at you. ['luk‿ət ju:]	Schaut euch an.
	to **take a photo** [ˌteɪk‿ə 'fəʊtəʊ]	ein Foto machen
	to **call** [kɔ:l]	rufen; anrufen
	to **hear** [hɪə]	hören
	them [ðem; ðəm]	sie *(Pl.)*; ihnen
	doorbell ['dɔ:bel]	Türklingel
	to **ring** [rɪŋ]	läuten; klingeln
	door [dɔ:]	Tür
	brilliant ['brɪliənt]	toll
	to **ask** [ɑ:sk]	fragen

Film corner

p. 83	**sleepover** ['sli:pˌəʊvə]	Übernachtung
	snack [snæk]	Snack; Imbiss
	to **like ... best** [ˌlaɪk 'best]	am meisten mögen; am liebsten mögen

1 Find the months. Finde die Monate.

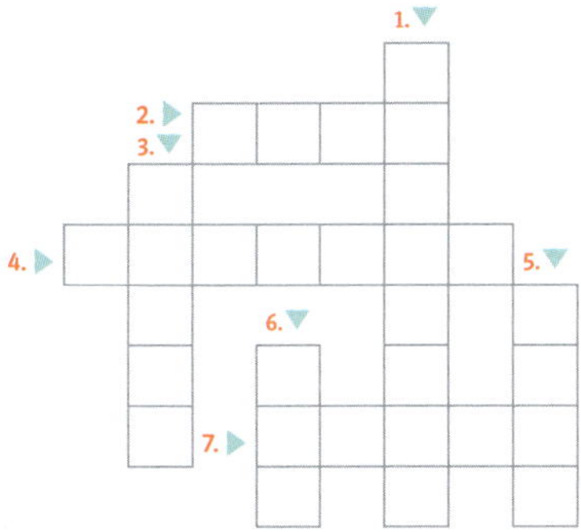

▶ 2. month number six
4. month number one
7. month number four

▼ 1. month number two
3. month number three
5. month number seven
6. month number five

2 Find more months. Finde weitere Monate.

a) Write them in English and German.
Schreibe sie in Englisch und Deutsch auf.

1. ____________________ ____________________
2. ____________________ ____________________
3. ____________________ ____________________
4. ____________________ ____________________
5. ____________________ ____________________

b) Write the right month. Schreibe den richtigen Monat auf.

1. Christmas: ____________ 2. New Year: ____________

3 Find the opposite. Finde das Gegenteil.

1. small ⟷ ______________________
2. always ⟷ ______________________
3. bad ⟷ ______________________
4. to get ⟷ ______________________

4 How often? Wie oft?

a) Find the words. Translate them. Put them in the right order.
Finde die Wörter, übersetze sie und sortiere sie von „immer“ bis „nie“.

veern ☹ → ______________________ ☐

wasayl ☺☺☺ → ______________________ [1]

siesmotem ☺ → ______________________ ☐

teonf ☺☺ → ______________________ ☐

b) Complete the sentences. Vervollständige die Sätze.

1. I ______________ (☺☺☺) get a cake on my birthday.

2. I ______________ (☺) get up late at the weekend.

3. I ______________ (☹) eat chocolate in our lessons.

4. I ______________ (☺☺) eat chocolate at home.

5 Match the parts. Ordne die Teile zu.

1. mi	late
2. sand	ge
3. oran	ke
4. choco	lk
5. ca	ese
6. che	wich

6 Is it food or not? Find the words and make a list in the chart. Ist es Essen oder nicht? Finde die Wörter und ordne sie in die Tabelle ein.

ttoleb • ledcan • lachocote • cspris • posh • garus • tubter • tapeck • geg • tun • albloon

Food	Not food

7 How do you say it in English?

Wie sagt man das auf Englisch?

1. Lasst uns feiern!

   ______________________________ !

2. Ich lade immer alle meine Freunde ein.

   I always ____________ all ______________________ .

3. Zuerst essen wir meinen Geburtstagskuchen.

   First we ______________________________ .

4. Dann gehen wir ins Kino.

   Then ______________________________ .

5. Am Abend machen wir eine Grillparty.

   In the ____________ we ______________________

   ______________________________ .

8 Write what you eat and do on your birthday.

Schreibe, wie du deinen Geburtstag feierst.

We eat ______________________________

______________________________ .

We ______________________________

______________________________ .

9 Find and write the words in English and German.

Finde die Wörter. Schreibe sie in Englisch und Deutsch auf.

1. ______________________ ______________________
2. ______________________ ______________________
3. ______________________ ______________________
4. ______________________ ______________________
5. ______________________ ______________________
6. ______________________ ______________________
7. ______________________ ______________________
8. ______________________ ______________________

10 Write the words. Schreibe die Wörter auf.

1.  ______________________
2.  ______________________
3.  ______________________
4.  ______________________

11 Write the words for the ordinal numbers.

Schreibe die Ordnungszahlen aus.

1st ______________________

2nd ______________________

9th ______________________

12th ______________________

20th ______________________

100th ______________________

12 Number and draw. Nummeriere und zeichne.

a) Write ordinal numbers under the boxes.
Nummeriere die Kästchen.

____*st* box	______ box	______ box	______ box

b) Read and draw the things in the right box.
Lies, dann male den Gegenstand in das richtige Kästchen.

Draw a banana in the first box. Draw a nose in the third box. Draw a CD in the fourth box. Draw clothes in the second box.

13 What are the party words? Welche Party-Wörter sind es?

a) Find the words (→ ↓). Finde die Wörter (→ ↓).

T	K	D	P	A	C	K	E	T	B	S
S	T	B	A	K	L	A	M	N	O	L
T	A	F	B	E	T	C	A	E	X	E
O	K	T	T	N	A	H	U	C	A	E
R	T	X	H	H	I	R	C	A	E	P
Y	B	R	I	L	L	I	A	N	T	O
B	A	J	N	C	U	S	R	D	C	V
S	M	N	G	B	O	T	T	L	E	E
N	I	T	S	I	H	M	B	E	I	R
A	A	E	Y	O	D	A	T	E	N	O
C	S	C	A	R	Y	S	W	E	E	T
K	I	N	V	I	T	A	T	I	O	N

b) Write the words down. Schreibe die Wörter auf.

→ 1. p ______	↓ 8. s ______
2. b ______	9. s ______
3. b ______	10. t ______
4. d ______	11. C ______
5. s ______	12. c ______
6. s ______	13. b ______
7. i ______	14. s ______

●14 Find the wrong word.

Finde das Wort, das nicht in die Reihe passt.

1. smurf • alien • narrator • dance
2. burger • ice cream • present • pasta
3. strawberry • flour • peach • orange
4. lemonade • milk • biscuit • coke
5. doorbell • superman • witch • pirate
6. can • carnival • bottle • packet

●15 Complete the sentences. Vervollständige die Sätze.

1. I'd like a bottle of ______________________________ .
2. Oh, and let's buy a box of ______________________________ .
3. Can I have a bar of ______________________________, please?
4. We also need some fruit. Can you buy some ______________

   ______________________________ ?
5. I'd like a can of ______________________________ .
6. I need a packet of ______________________________ .

Unit 5 Where I live

Way in

town

flat [flæt]	Wohnung	**café** ['kæfeɪ]	Café
road [rəʊd]	Straße	**park** [pɑ:k]	Park
house [haʊs]	Haus	**station** ['steɪʃn]	Bahnhof
swimming pool ['swɪmɪŋ ˌpu:l]	Schwimmbad	**library** ['laɪbri]	Bibliothek; Bücherei
shopping centre ['ʃɒpɪŋ ˌsentə]	Einkaufszentrum	**department store** [dɪ'pɑ:tmənt ˌstɔ:]	Kaufhaus
		market ['mɑ:kɪt]	Markt
sports shop ['spɔ:ts ˌʃɒp]	Sportgeschäft	**museum** [mju:'zi:əm]	Museum
shop [ʃɒp]	Geschäft; Laden	**supermarket** ['su:pəˌmɑ:kɪt]	Supermarkt
post office ['pəʊst‿ˌɒfɪs]	Postamt	**river** ['rɪvə]	Fluss

p. 90	to **live** [lɪv]	wohnen; leben
	town [taʊn]	Stadt
	ship [ʃɪp]	Schiff
p. 91	to **take** [teɪk]	nehmen; mitnehmen
	to **go swimming** [ˌgəʊ 'swɪmɪŋ]	schwimmen gehen

Station 1

p. 92	**morning** ['mɔ:nɪŋ]	Morgen; Vormittag
	tired [taɪəd]	müde
	yesterday ['jestədeɪ]	gestern

	was [wɒz]	simple past von *to be* (sein)
	exciting [ɪk'saɪtɪŋ]	spannend; aufregend
	won [wʌn]	simple past von *to win* (gewinnen)
	Guess what? [ges 'wɒt]	Weißt du was?
	saw [sɔ:]	simple past von *to see* (sehen)
	bought [bɔ:t]	simple past von *to buy* (kaufen)
	went [went]	simple past von *to go* (gehen)
	last [lɑ:st]	letzte/-r/-s
	had [hæd]	simple past von *to have* (haben, essen); simple past von *to have* (haben, essen)
	pizza ['pi:tsə]	Pizza
	did [dɪd]	simple past von *to do* (machen, tun)
	to **do homework** [ˌdu: 'həʊmwɜ:k]	Hausaufgabe(n) machen
	to **tell** [tel], **told** [təʊld]	erzählen; sagen
p. 94	**about** [ə'baʊt]	über
	to visit ['vɪzɪt]	besuchen
p. 95	**made** [meɪd]	simple past von *to make* (machen)
	boring ['bɔ:rɪŋ]	langweilig

Manche Wörter prägen sich besser durch Beispielsätze ein. Überlege dir deine eigenen Beispielsätze:

We won our game!
I love pizza.
I was tired yesterday.
But I did my homework!

Station 2

transport

train [treɪn]	Zug	**helicopter** ['helɪkɒptə]	Helikopter; Hub-schrauber
car [kɑ:]	Auto	**plane** [pleɪn]	Flugzeug
ship [ʃɪp]	Schiff	**boat** [bəʊt]	Boot
bus [bʌs]	Bus	**motorbike** ['məʊtəbaɪk]	Motorrad
bike [baɪk]	Fahrrad	**skateboard** ['skeɪtbɔ:d]	Skateboard
submarine [ˌsʌbmr'i:n]	U-Boot	**underground** ['ʌndəgraʊnd]	U-Bahn
tram [træm]	Straßen-bahn		

p. 96	**trip** [trɪp]	Ausflug
	at the seaside [ət ðə 'si:saɪd]	am Meer
	It's two hours from here. [ɪts tu: 'aʊəz frɒm ˌhɪə]	Es ist zwei Stunden von hier entfernt.
	by (train) [baɪ]	mit (dem Zug)
	to **get lost** [get lɒst], **got lost** [gɒt lɒst]	sich verirren
	on the way [ˌɒn ðə ˌ'weɪ]	auf dem Weg; unterwegs
	forgot [fə'gɒt]	simple past von *to forget* (vergessen)
	satnav ['sætnæv]	Navi
	Oh dear! [ˌəʊ 'dɪə]	Oje!
	sea [si:]	Meer
	water ['wɔ:tə]	Wasser
	cold [kəʊld]	kalt
	beach [bi:tʃ]	Strand
	frisbee ['frɪzbi]	Frisbee; Frisbeescheibe
	chips *(pl)* [tʃɪps]	Pommes frites
	vegetarian [ˌvedʒɪ'teəriən]	Vegetarier; Vegetarierin

	were [wɜː]	simple past von *to be* (sein)
	postcard ['pəʊstkɑːd]	Postkarte
	to **send** [send], **sent** [sent]	schicken; senden
p. 97	**on foot** [ɒn 'fʊt]	zu Fuß
	most [məʊst]	die meisten; die Mehrheit
	no one ['nəʊ wʌn]	niemand
p. 98	**to see friends** [siː 'frendz]	Freunde treffen
p. 99	**ice cream** [ˌaɪs 'kriːm]	Eiscreme; Eis
	theme park ['θiːm ˌpɑːk]	Freizeitpark

Reading corner

p. 100	**adventure** [əd'ventʃə]	Abenteuer
	attic ['ætɪk]	Dachboden
	diary ['daɪəri]	Tagebuch
	great-great-grandad [ˌgreɪt greɪt 'grændæd]	Ururopa
	today [tə'deɪ]	heute
	job [dʒɒb]	Job
	Australia [ɒs'treɪliə]	Australien
	to **hate** [heɪt]	hassen; nicht mögen
	to be sick [bi 'sɪk]	sich übergeben
	first mate [ˌfɜːst 'meɪt]	erster Offizier
	awful ['ɔːfl]	schrecklich; furchtbar
	to throw [θrəʊ], threw [θruː]	werfen
	bucket of water ['bʌkɪt‿əv ˌwɔːtə]	Eimer Wasser
	over ['əʊvə]	über
	potato *(sg)* [pə'teɪtəʊ], **potatoes** *(pl)* [pə'teɪtəʊz]	Kartoffel
p. 101	**storm** [stɔːm]	Sturm
	wave [weɪv]	Welle
	shout [ʃaʊt]	Schrei
	Man overboard! [mæn 'əʊvəbɔːd]	Mann über Bord!

	man *(sg)* [mæn], **men** *(pl)* [men]	Mann
	rope [rəʊp]	Seil
	beautiful ['bju:tɪfl]	schön; hübsch
	shark [ʃɑ:k]	Hai
	bag [bæg]	Sack
	sheep *(sg)* [ʃi:p], **sheep** *(pl)* [ʃi:p]	Schaf
	life *(sg)* [laɪf], **lives** *(pl)* [laɪvz]	Leben
p. 100	**found** [faʊnd]	simple past von *to find* (finden)
	wrote [rəʊt]	simple past von *to write* (schreiben)
p. 101	**put** [pʊt]	simple past von *to put* (stellen, setzen, legen)

Film corner

p. 103	**out and about** [ˌaʊt‿ən‿ə'baʊt]	unterwegs
	popcorn ['pɒpkɔ:n]	Popcorn
	post office ['pəʊst‿ˌɒfɪs]	Postamt
	back [bæk]	zurück

Speaking skills

p. 108	**asking the way** ['ɑ:skɪŋ ðə ˌweɪ]	nach dem Weg fragen
	tourist ['tʊərɪst]	Tourist; Touristin
	Can you tell me the way to …? [kæn ju: 'tel mi ðə ˌweɪ tə]	Kannst du mir sagen, wie ich nach … komme?
	Tourist Information Centre ['tʊərɪst ɪnfə'meɪʃn ˌsentə]	Touristeninformation
	along [ə'lɒŋ]	entlang
	straight on [streɪt‿'ɒn]	geradeaus
	to turn right [ˌtɜ:n 'raɪt]	(nach) rechts abbiegen
	at the end of the road [ət ði: 'end‿əv ðə ˌrəʊd]	am Ende der Straße

	on the left [ɒn ðə 'left]	auf der linken Seite; links
	on the right [ɒn ðə 'raɪt]	auf der rechten Seite; rechts
	opposite ['ɒpəzɪt]	gegenüber
	until [ʌn'tɪl]	bis
	to **turn left** [ˌtɜːn 'left]	(nach) links abbiegen
p. 109	**hospital** ['hɒspɪtl]	Hospital; Krankenhaus

Lerne nicht zu viele Wörter auf einmal. Lerne lieber jeden Tag einige neue Wörter und wiederhole öfter, was du gelernt hast.

1 Match the words and write the places.

Ordne die Wörter zu und schreibe die Wortpaare auf.

1. swimming	centre	______________
2. shopping	room	______________
3. sports	office	______________
4. post	shop	______________
5. living	studio	______________
6. recording	pool	______________

2 Write the verbs in the simple past.

Schreibe die Vergangenheitsformen auf.

1. I ______________ (be) tired this morning.
2. We ______________ (win) the game.
3. She ______________ (see) a friend.
4. You ______________ (buy) a CD.
5. They ______________ (go) to school at 9 o'clock.
6. I ______________ (have) a pizza.
7. She ______________ (tell) us a story.
8. We ______________ (do) our homework.
9. I ______________ (make) a poster with photos of our school trip.

3 Write the words. Schreibe die Wörter auf.

1. 

____

2. 

____

3. 

____

4. 

____

5. 

____

6. 

____

7. 

____

8. 

____

9. 

4 Complete the sentences. Vervollständige die Sätze.

1. am Meer	He's ________ the ____________ .
2. auf den Weg	She's ________ the ____________
3. Oje!	home.
4. sich verirren	Oh ________________!
5. von hier	We often get __________ in London.
6. Weißt du was?	It's 2 hours __________ __________ .
7. schwimmen gehen	Guess ____________ ?
	I ______ ____________ after school.

5 Find the words. Finde die Wörter.

1. I don't like that food. It's ________________________ .
2. When's lunch? I'm very ________________________ .
3. I need my pullover. It's so ________________________ .
4. It's my birthday. I'm really ________________________ .
5. You're very ________________________ . Go to bed!
6. I love this beach. It's very ________________________ here.
7. This film is very ________________________ .

6 Choose the right word. Wähle das richtige Wort.

1. He lives ______ (in/at/on) the end ______ (in/to/of) the road.
2. Our house is ______ (in/at/on) the left.
3. Go straight ______ (at/in/on), then turn left into Bat Road.
4. Walk ___________ (along/in/at) this road.
5. We go to school ______ (by/on/to) foot.
6. Let's go ______ (by/on/to) bus.
7. There's a nice café ______ (by/in/on) the way to town.

7 Complete the sentences. Vervollständige die Sätze.

1. __________ ________ into Old Walk.

2. Our house is _____ ______ _________ .

3. The park is at _____________

_____________ of the road.

4. ________ _____________ into Park Road.

5. Go _______________ on past the café.

8 Put in the right verb forms.

Vervollständige die Tabelle mit den richtigen Verbformen.

German	English (infinitive)	Simple past
1. sich verirren	____________	____________
2. ____________	to send	____________
3. ____________	____________	was, were
4. kaufen	____________	____________
5. ____________	to go	____________
6. ____________	____________	told

9 Match the sentence parts. Ordne die Satzteile zu.

1. Can you tell me	a) come back for it later?
2. Excuse	b) out and about in London.
3. The sea is two hours	c) the Tourist Information Centre.
4. Ah, my present! Can I	d) can I there by bus then?
5. My dad's on	e) from here!
6. Guess	f) the way to Greenwich, please?
7. Today we're	g) me. Where's the post office?
8. The café is opposite	h) what?
9. What, no trains? Well,	i) his way here.

●10 Write the opposite. Schreibe das Gegenteil auf.

1. to love ____________
2. good ____________
3. right ____________
4. new ____________
5. great ____________
6. evening ____________

●11 Write the words in English or German.

Schreibe die Wörter auf Englisch oder Deutsch.

1. ____________ Boot
2. plane ____________
3. ____________ U-Boot
4. helicopter ____________
5. ____________ Straßenbahn
6. motorbike ____________
7. ____________ U-Bahn

●12 Write the words. Schreibe die Wörter auf.

1.  ____________

2.  ____________

3.  ____________

4.  ____________

●13 Complete the answers. Vervollständige die Antworten.

1. What do some people write in every day? In a __________ .
2. Who is your dad's dad's dad's dad? He's your __________

   __________________ .

3. What do people get from a sheep?

   They get __________________ .
4. Where can you find lots of trains? In the __________ .
5. Who does the captain's job when he or she is sick?

   The __________________ .
6. Where can you get books (not a shop)? In the __________ .

●14 Plurals. Die Mehrzahl.

a) Write the plurals.
Schreibe die Mehrzahl.

b) Write them in German.
Schreibe sie auf Deutsch.

	a)	b)
1. life	__________	__________
2. man	__________	__________
3. sheep	__________	__________
4. diary	__________	__________
5. adventure	__________	__________

Unit 6 A trip to the country

Way in

p. 110	**country** ['kʌntri]	ländliche Gegend; Land
	farm [fɑ:m]	Bauernhof
	school trip [ˌsku:l 'trɪp]	Klassenfahrt
	holiday ['hɒlədeɪ]	Ferien; Urlaub
	in the country [ɪn ðə 'kʌntri]	auf dem Land
	to meet [mi:t], **met** [met]	kennen lernen
	us [ʌs]	wir; uns
	farmer ['fɑ:mə]	Landwirt; Landwirtin; Bauer; Bäuerin
	daughter ['dɔ:tə]	Tochter
	chicken ['tʃɪkɪn]	Huhn
p. 111	**modern** ['mɒdn]	modern
	GPS ***(Global Positioning System)*** [ˌdʒi:pi:'es]	GPS
	collar ['kɒlə]	Halsband
	tractor ['træktə]	Traktor
	near [nɪə]	in der Nähe von
	rock climbing ['rɒk ˌklaɪmɪŋ]	Klettern
	canoeing [kə'nu:ɪŋ]	Kanufahren
	needn't ['ni:dnt]	nicht brauchen; nicht müssen
	to worry ['wʌri]	sich Sorgen machen
	came [keɪm]	simple past von *to come* (kommen)
	to click [klɪk]	klicken
p. 110	**fed** [fed]	simple past von *to feed* (füttern)
p. 111	**Would you like (to) ...?** [ˌwʊd jə 'laɪk (tə)]	Möchtest du ...?
	I'd like (to) ... (= I would like to) [aɪd 'laɪk (tə)]	Ich möchte ...; Ich würde gerne ...
	I wouldn't like (to) ... [aɪ 'wʊdnt laɪk (tə)]	Ich möchte nicht ...; Ich würde nicht gerne ...

Station 1

clothes

coat [kəʊt]	Jacke	**T-shirt** ['ti:ʃɜ:t]	T-Shirt
trousers *(pl)* ['traʊzəz]	Hose; Hosen	**scarf** *(sg)* [skɑ:f], **scarves** *(pl)* [skɑ:vz]	Schal; Tuch
shoe [ʃu:]	Schuh	**trainer** ['treɪnə]	Turnschuh
sock [sɒk]	Socke	**shorts** *(pl)* [ʃɔ:ts]	Shorts; kurze Hose
sweatshirt ['swetʃɜ:t]	Sweat-shirt	**cap** [kæp]	Kappe; Mütze
jeans *(pl)* [dʒi:nz]	Jeans	**blouse** [blaʊz]	Bluse
skirt [skɜ:t]	Rock	**top** [tɒp]	Top
shirt [ʃɜ:t]	Hemd; Shirt		
dress [dres]	Kleid		

p. 112	**phone call** ['fəʊn ˌkɔ:l]	Telefonanruf
	How are you? [ˌhaʊ‿'ɑ: jə]	Wie geht es dir?
	arm [ɑ:m]	Arm
	better ['betə]	besser
	horse riding ['hɔ:s ˌraɪdɪŋ]	Reiten
	picnic ['pɪknɪk]	Picknick
	group [gru:p]	Gruppe
	must [mʌst]	müssen
	to stop [stɒp]	aufhören
	night walk [ˌnaɪt 'wɔ:k]	Nachtwanderung
	warm [wɔ:m]	warm
	See you soon! ['si: ju ˌsu:n]	Bis bald!
p. 113	**colourful** ['kʌləfl]	bunt
	chic [ʃɪk]	schick; elegant
	pretty ['prɪti]	hübsch

p. 114	**broke** [brəʊk]	simple past von *to break* (brechen)
	poor [pɔ:; pʊə]	arm
p. 115	**alone** [ə'ləʊn]	allein
	What happened? [ˌwɒt 'hæpnd]	Was ist geschehen?; Was ist passiert?
	test [test]	Test; Klassenarbeit
	terrible ['terəbl]	schrecklich; schlimm; furchtbar

Station 2

weather

sunny ['sʌni]	sonnig	**cold** [kəʊld]	kalt
hot [hɒt]	heiß	**foggy** ['fɒgi]	neblig
to rain [reɪn]	regnen	**mild** [maɪld]	mild
wet [wet]	nass	**dry** [draɪ]	trocken
windy ['wɪndi]	windig	**cool** [ku:l]	kühl
cloudy ['klaʊdi]	wolkig	**rainy** ['reɪni]	regnerisch
warm [wɔ:m]	warm	**fine** [faɪn]	schön

to **go on a night walk** [ˌgəʊ ɒn‿ə 'naɪt wɔ:k]	eine Nachtwanderung machen
torch [tɔ:tʃ]	Taschenlampe
dark [dɑ:k]	dunkel
heard [hɜ:d]	simple past von *to hear* (hören)
to **get** [get], **got** [gɒt]	werden
wet [wet]	nass
because [bɪ'kɒz]	weil; da
Best wishes [ˌbest 'wɪʃɪz]	Viele Grüße
Devon ['devn]	*Grafschaft in Südwestengland*
Any idea? [ˌeni aɪ'dɪə]	Irgendeine Idee?

p. 117	**What's the weather like?** [ˌwɒts ðə 'weðə laɪk]	Wie ist das Wetter?
	idea [aɪ'dɪə]	Idee; Ahnung
p. 118	**in time** [ɪn 'taɪm]	rechtzeitig
p. 119	**to hope** [həʊp]	hoffen
	to say hi to [ˌseɪ 'haɪ tə]	grüßen; Grüße ausrichten
	earlier ['ɜ:liə]	früher
	Take care. ['teɪk ˌkeə]	Macht's gut.

Reading corner

p. 120	**to be stuck** [bi 'stʌk]	feststecken; nicht weg können
	mud [mʌd]	Schlamm; Matsch
	to meet [mi:t], **met** [met]	treffen
	wheelchair ['wi:ltʃeə]	Rollstuhl
	said [sed]	simple past von *to say* (sagen)
	to point (at) [ˌpɔɪnt‿'ət]	zeigen (auf)
	laptop ['læptɒp]	Laptop
	to answer ['ɑ:nsə]	antworten; beantworten
	all alone [ˌɔ:l‿ə'ləʊn]	ganz allein
	river ['rɪvə]	Fluss
	isn't answering his mobile [ɪznt 'ɑ:nsərɪŋ hɪz ˌməʊbaɪl]	geht nicht an sein Handy
p. 121	**thought** [θɔ:t]	simple past von *to think* (denken)
	muddy ['mʌdi]	schlammig
	welly ['weli]	Gummistiefel
	to get [get], **got** [gɒt]	holen
	Come on! [ˌkʌm‿'ɒn]	Komm jetzt!
	line [laɪn]	Linie
	to push [pʊʃ]	schieben; drücken
	from behind [ˌfrəm bɪ'haɪnd]	von hinten
	to pull [pʊl]	ziehen
	side [saɪd]	Seite

	still [stɪl]	noch; immer noch
	clean [kli:n]	sauber
	foot *(sg)* [fʊt], **feet** *(pl)* [fi:t]	Fuß
	out of ['aʊt‿əv]	aus ... heraus
	to fall [fɔ:l], fell [fel]	fallen

Film corner

p. 123	**cache box** ['kæʃ ˌbɒks]	*Schatzkiste beim Geocaching*
	geocaching ['dʒiəʊkæʃɪŋ]	Geocaching
	cache [kæʃ]	Cache *(Geheimschatz)*

Es hilft dir beim Vokabellernen Wörter zu einem bestimmten Thema zusammenzufassen. Mach dir ein Poster und hänge es in deinem Zimmer auf:

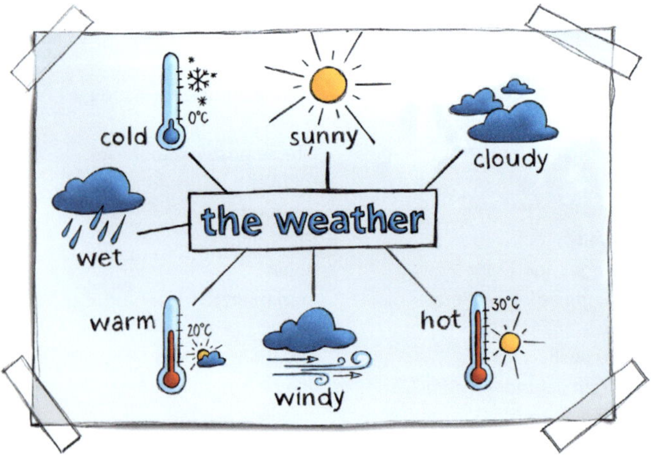

1 **Write the words.** Schreibe die Wörter auf.

1. ______________________ 2. ______________________

3. ______________ 5. ______________

4. ______________ 7. ______________

6. ______________

2 **Write the wrong word.** Schreibe das falsche Wort auf.

1. came • fed • worry • met ______________
2. scary • modern • boring • country ______________
3. holiday • farmer • school trip • click ______________
4. canoeing • exciting • climbing • swimming ______________
5. GPS • near • collar • sheep ______________

3 Complete the dialogue. Vervollständige den Dialog.

A: Would you ______________ to be a farmer?

B: No, but ______________ like to have a holiday on a farm.

A: Yes, on a farm there are lots of ______________:

sheep, horses and chickens. You can ______________ the

chickens and eat their ______________.

B: Yes, that's cool for a week or two. But I ______________

like to be a farmer because they must work all day.

4 What can you wear? Write down the words.

Schreibe die Kleidungswörter auf.

T -	S	H	I	R	T	J
X	L	N	S	Y	R	E
V	S	H	O	E	O	A
A	K	C	C	C	U	N
J	I	O	K	B	S	S
T	R	A	I	N	E	R
N	T	T	Z	E	R	D
S	C	A	R	F	S	A

____

____

5 Find the words. Finde die Wörter.

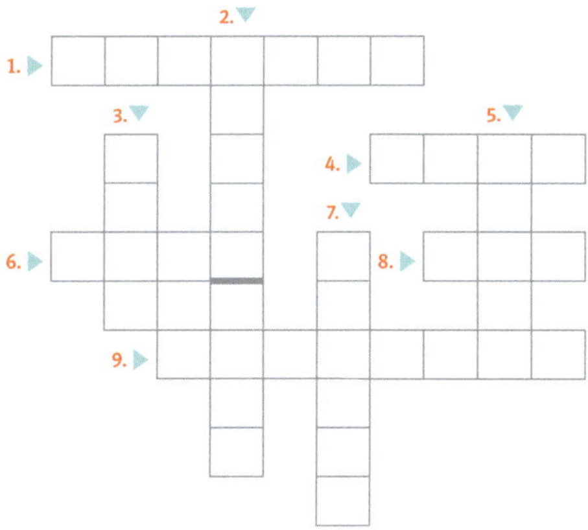

▶ across

1. I live in the … not the town.
4. I … it's dry tomorrow. We want to go climbing.
6. good – better – …
8. cold ↔ …
9. You're late! What …? – We got lost!

▼ down

2. It's an activity: out and about at night.
3. I … my friends in the park and at school.
5. She wants to make a … call on her mobile.
7. It's a computer you can take with you.

6 Complete the dialogue. Vervollständige den Dialog.

Helen: Pupils from Greenwich High School want to g__________ on a night walk tonight, Geoff. M__________ they take their scarves with them?

Geoff: No, Helen. They're lucky! It's h__________ and s__________ in London now and they needn't worry about the weather later.

Helen: And what's the w__________ like in other places today?

Geoff: Well, it isn't too bad in England. It's cl__________ but it isn't c__________. People aren't so lucky in Wales b__________ there it's w__________ and very w__________.

7 Find the word pairs. Put them in the sentences.

Finde die Wortpaare. Schreibe sie in den richtigen Sätzen.

1. __________ is the opposite of __________ .
2. We say one __________ but two __________ .
3. __________ is the simple past of __________ .
4. You can go __________ on a __________ .

8 Write the simple past.

Schreibe die Vergangenheitsform auf.

1. fall ____________________
2. meet ____________________
3. hear ____________________
4. go ____________________
5. get ____________________
6. say ____________________

9 Find the 12 words. Write them in the chart.

Finde die zwölf Wörter. Schreibe sie in die Tabelle.

S	H	O	R	T	S	M	I	L	D
F	B	L	O	U	S	E	M	B	L
O	S	T	U	R	I	D	I	N	G
G	E	O	C	A	C	H	I	N	G
G	I	P	A	C	O	O	L	U	D
Y	A	G	P	X	P	A	D	R	Y
B	A	S	K	E	T	B	A	L	L
R	C	C	A	N	O	E	I	N	G

Weather	Clothes	Hobbies
____________	____________	horse r____________
____________	____________	____________
____________	____________	____________
____________	____________	____________

●10 Match the words and translate into German.

Ordne die Wörter zu und übersetze ins Deutsche.

1. I'm careful! ______ ______
2. Well on. ______ ______
3. Be stuck! ______ ______
4. Any done! ______ ______
5. Come idea? ______ ______

●11 Write the words. Schreibe die Wörter auf.

1.  ______
2.  ______
3.  ______
4. 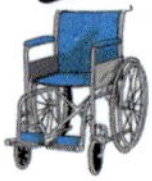 ______

●12 Find the words. Write them down.

Finde die Wörter und schreibe sie an der richtigen Stelle auf.

ringbo • cchi • ourfulcol • ttrepy • demorn • sacry

1. This isn't black or white. ______
2. She looks good. ______
3. It's not old. ______
4. This film is more than exciting. ______
5. It's the opposite of exciting. ______
6. The trousers look good. ______

Welcome – Hello/Zoom in – In a park

1 Hello, I'm Jonas. What's your name? / My name is Elena. Nice to meet you. / It's time to go. / Yes. See you later.
2 Hello!/Hi! My name is .... I like sport/animals/music. Goodbye!/Bye!
3 1. I like English. 2. I like music. 3. I like my computer. 4. I like Ben (the bat). 5. I like sport/football.
4 1. three, 2. eight, 3. seven, 4. five, 5. six, 6. nine, 7. eight
5 1. sport, 2. people, 3. number, 4. park, 5. colour, 6. activity
6 1. park, 2. black, 3. cool, 4. play, 5. something, 6. tennis, 7. activities
7 red, yellow, pink, purple, orange, grey, blue, black, brown, green, white
8 1. purple, 2. green, 3. orange, 4. white, 5. pink, 6. brown

Unit 1

1 1. mother/mum, 2. father/dad, 3. brother, 4. sister
● 2 uncle, aunt, grandmother, grandfather, cousin, parents
3 1. his sister, 2. her brother, 3. my friend, 4. our family
4 1. table, 2. chair, 3. bed, 4. shelf, 5. shelves
5 1. house, 2. happy, 3. problem, 4. great, 5. dream, 6. night, 7. busy, 8. tree
6 1. kitchen, 2. bathroom, 3. bedroom, 4. dining room, 5. living room, 6. garden
7 individuelle Lösung
8 1. on, 2. next to, 3. under, 4. next to, 5. in
● 9 1. lamp – Lampe, 2. bed – Bett, 3. wardrobe – Kleiderschrank, 4. trainer – Turnschuh, 5. book – Buch, 6. computer – Computer, 7. table – Tisch
● 10 1. noise, 2. parents, 3. uncle, 4. wood, 5. alarm clock, 6. ladder, 7. tree house, 8. lunch

Unit 2

1 1. eat, 2. can go, 3. can open, 4. can sing, 5. can dance, 6. can talk

2 1. year – Jahr, 2. uniform – Uniform, 3. school – school, 4. place – Platz, 5. playground – Schulhof, 6. teacher – Lehrer

3 1. pen, 2. eraser, 3. ruler, 4. exercise book, 5. bag , 6. pencil

4 1. red pencil, 2. write, 3. an eraser, 4. sit, 5. Open , 6. exercise book

5 1. week, 2. singer, 3. classroom, 4. very, 5. window, 6. talent show, 7. please, 8. really, 9. recording studio, 10. tutor

6 1. boy – girl, 2. hand – finger, 3. teacher – student, 4. question – answer, 5. singer – song, 6. open – close

7 1. an, 2. a, 3. an, 4. a, 5. a, 6. a, 7. an, 8. an, 9. a, 10. an

8 1. play, 2. talk/listen, 3. sit, 4. listen, 5. do, 6. say, 7. write, 8. look

9 1. Thursday, Design Technology, 2. Tuesday, Friday 3. Monday, Maths, 4. Wednesday

10 1. French, 2. Physical Education, 3. German, 4. Saturday, Sunday, 5. Music

11 1. timetable, 2. subject, 3. spelling, 4. alphabet, 5. joke 6. lesson

12 1. You're right. 2. Ich bin gut in Französisch.
3. Du schließt Freundschaften. 4. I like chewing gum.
5. Can you spell that, please?

● 13 1. langweilig (boring), 2. Gewinner (winner), 3. Saxophon (saxophone), 4. Restaurant (restaurant), 5. schwierig (difficult)

● 14 School things: calculator, glue, felt-tip, pencil case, pen
School subjects: Information, Technology, Geography, Maths, History, RE, PE

Unit 3

1 1. cinema, 2. netball, 3. free time, 4. football practice, 5. team, 6. watch, 7. Every, run

2 1. captain – Kapitän/Kapitänin, 2. famous – berühmt, 3. around – herum/umher, 4. programme – Programme/ Sendung, 5. lunchtime – Mittagspause/Mittagszeit, 6. after – nach

3 1. watch TV – fernsehen, 2. help – helfen, 3. love – lieben, 4. run – rennen, 5. win – gewinnen, 6. want – wollen, 7. come – kommen

4 1. bear, 2. bird, 3. parrot, 4. horse, 5. elephant, 6. snake

5 24, 88, 30, 63, 29, 58, 100, 12

6 1. sixteen, 2. twenty-five, 3. twelve, 4. ninety, 5. twenty, 6. seventeen, 7. ninety-nine, 8. forty

7 a) 1. grass, 2. bananas, 3. meat, 4. fruit, 5. mice, 6. plants
b) 1. grass, 2. bananas, 3. meat, 4. A parrot eats fruit. 5. A snake eats mice. 6. An elephant eats plants.

8 1. The zookeeper gets up. 2. He eats a banana for breakfast. 3. He goes/walks to the zoo. 4. First he feeds the penguins. 5. After that he plays with the monkey. 6. Their cages are dirty. 7. He cleans their cages. 8. He loves his work. 9. He is in the zoo for nine hours a day.

9 a) + b) 1. meat – Fleisch, 2. why – warum, 3. afternoon – Nachmittag, 4. also – auch, 5. story – Geschichte, 6. mystery – Rätsel/Geheimnis, 7. interview – Interview, 8. long – lang, 9. small – klein, 10. magazine – Zeitschrift, 11. only – nur, 12. work – Arbeit; arbeiten, 13. how – wie, 14. age – Alter

10 1. 10:30, 2. 4:15, 3. 7:45, 4. 8:50

● 11 1. one fifteen, 2. ten past three, 3. It's five thirty, 4. It's eight forty-five, a quarter to nine 5. It's ten fifteen, a quarter past ten

Unit 4

1 → 2. June, 4. January, 7. April,
↓ 1. February, 3. March, 5. July, 6. May

2 a) 1. August – August, 2. September – September, 3. October – Oktober, 4. November – November 5. December – Dezember
b) 1. December, 2. January

3 1. small ↔ big, 2. always ↔ never, 3. bad ↔ good 4. to get ↔ to give

4 a) 1. always – immer, 2. often – oft, 3. sometimes – manchmal, 4. never – nie
b) 1. always, 2. sometimes, 3. never, 4. often

5 milch, sandwich, orange, chocolate, cake, cheese

6 Food: chocolate, crisps, sugar, butter, egg, nut
Not food: candle, shop, packet, bottle, balloon

7 1. Let's celebrate! 2. I always invite all my friends.
3. First we eat my birthday cake. 4. Then we go to the cinema. 5. In the evening we have a barbeque party.

8 Musterlösung: We eat chocolate cake, fruit, sweets, crisps and sandwiches. We go to the park/cinema, watch movies, play games, have a barbeque party ...

9 1. present – Geschenk, 2. surprise – Überraschung, 3. cute – süß/niedlich, 4. everyone – jede(r)/alle, 5. packet – Packung/Tüte, 6. candle – Kerze, 7. together – zusammen, 8. costume – Kostüm

10 1. bottle, 2. balloon, 3. box, 4. money

11 first, second, ninth, twelfth, twentieth, hundredth

12 1st: banana, 2nd: clothes, 3rd: nose, 4th: CD

13 1. packet, 2. brilliant, 3. bottle, 4. date, 5. scary, 6. sweet
7. invitation, 8. story, 9. snack, 10. things, 11. Christmas,
12. candle, 13. box, 14. sleepover

● 14 1. dance, 2. present, 3. flour, 4. biscuit, 5. doorbell,
6. carnival

● 15 1. milk/water/lemonade/coke, 2. eggs/chocolates, 3. chocolate,
4. apples/bananas/oranges, 5. tomatoes/peaches/pet food,
6. biscuits/tea/candles/balloons/crisps

Unit 5

1 1. swimming pool, 2. shopping centre, 3. sports shop,
4. post office, 5. living room, 6. recording studio

2 1. was, 2. won, 3. saw, 4. bought, 5. went, 6. had, 7. told,
8. did, 9. made

3 1. train, 2. car, 3. chips, 4. bus, 5. bike, 6. ship, 7. beach,
8. sea, 9. house

4 1. at, seaside, 2. on, way, 3. dear, 4. lost, 5. from here,
6. what, 7. go swimming

5 1. awful, 2. hungry, 3. cold, 4. happy, 5. tired, 6. beautiful,
7. exciting

6 1. at, of, 2. on, 3. on, 4. along, 5. on, 6. by, 7. on